CHILDREN'S LIBRARY

word building

Playing Sports

Word Building with Prefixes and Suffixes

Pam Scheunemann

Consulting Editor, Diane Craig, M.A./Reading Specialist

A Division of ABDO
ABDO
Publishing Company

visit us at www.abdopublishing.com

Published by ABDO Publishing Company, a division of ABDO, P.O. Box 398166, Minneapolis, Minnesota 55439. Copyright © 2013 by Abdo Consulting Group, Inc. International copyrights reserved in all countries. No part of this book may be reproduced in any form without written permission from the publisher. Super SandCastle™ is a trademark and logo of ABDO Publishing Company.

Printed in the United States of America, North Mankato, Minnesota
062012
092012

 PRINTED ON RECYCLED PAPER

Editor: Liz Salzmann
Content Developer: Nancy Tuminelly
Interior Design: Kelly Doudna, Mighty Media, Inc.
Production: Oona Gaarder-Juntti, Mighty Media, Inc.
Photo Credits: Brand X Pictures, Comstock Images, George Doyle, Hermera Technologies, Jupiterimages, Polka Dot images, Shutterstock, Thinkstock Images

Library of Congress Cataloging-in-Publication Data
Scheunemann, Pam, 1955-
  Playing sports : word building with prefixes and suffixes / Pam Scheunemann.
    p. cm. -- (Word building)
  ISBN 978-1-61714-971-9
  1. English language--Suffixes and prefixes--Juvenile literature. 2. Vocabulary--Juvenile literature. 3. Language arts (Elementary) I. Title.
  PE1175.S3466 2012
  428.1--dc22
                              2010054484

Super SandCastle™ books are created by a team of professional educators, reading specialists, and content developers around five essential components—phonemic awareness, phonics, vocabulary, text comprehension, and fluency—to assist young readers as they develop reading skills and strategies and increase their general knowledge. All books are written, reviewed, and leveled for guided reading, early reading intervention, and Accelerated Reader® programs for use in shared, guided, and independent reading and writing activities to support a balanced approach to literacy instruction.

contents

what is word building?

Word building is adding groups of letters to a word. The added letters change the word's meaning.

view s

Prefix

Some groups of letters are added to the beginning of words. They are called prefixes. Some prefixes have more than one meaning.

Suffix

Some groups of letters are added to the end of words. They are called suffixes. Some suffixes have more than one meaning.

re + view + ing
prefix + base word + suffix

reviewing

The prefix **re** means to do it again.
The base word **view** means to look at.
The suffix **ing** means that the action is happening now.
Reviewing means someone is looking at something again.

Let's Build words

tie

Alyssa likes to tie her skates together.

Jason sits down to retie his shoe.

Tamika's shoe is untied.

retie

The prefix **re** means to do it again.

untied

The prefix **un** means not or opposite.

The suffix **ed** turns a word into an adjective.

More Words

ties, tied, retying, untie, unties, untying, tying

～ ～ ～ RULE ～ ～ ～

When a verb ends with *e*, drop the *e* before adding **ed**.

run

Jane can run very fast.

David's favorite sport is running.

Michael reruns the relay race.

running

The suffix **ing** turns a verb into a noun.

rerun**s**

The prefix **re** means to do it again.

The suffix **s** means that the action is happening now.

More Words

runs, runner, runners, rerun, rerunning

win

Tara's team needs one more out to win the game.

Sam hopes to rewin the trophy for a third time.

Billy's team is winning the game.

rewin

The prefix **re** means to do it again.

winn**ing**

The suffix **ing** means that the action is happening now.

More words

wins, winner, winless, winnable, unwinnable

safe

Jarrett is safe at home plate.

Amy knows it is unsafe to skate without a helmet.

Grace and Bryan know where they can ride safely.

unsafe

The prefix **un** means not or opposite.

safely

The suffix **ly** changes the word to mean how something is done.

More Words

safer, safest, safeness, safety, unsafely

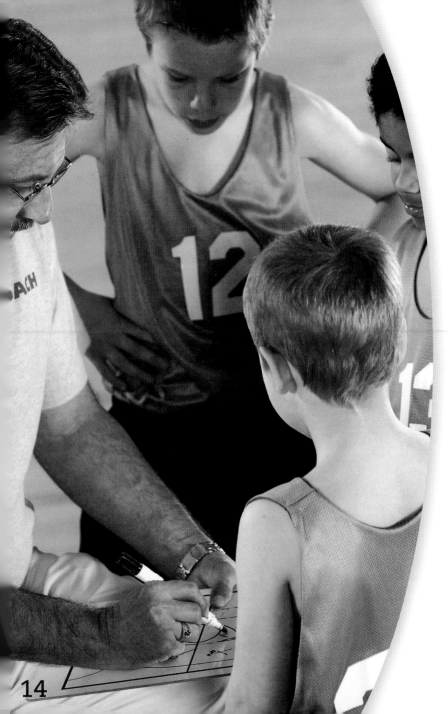

look

The team looks at a play during a time-out.

Tony knows to look at the basket when he shoots the ball.

Taylor is looking at her horse.

looks

The suffix **s** means that the action is happening now.

looking

The suffix **ing** means that the action is happening now.

More Words

looker, looked, relooked, relooking

The Unknown Ballplayer

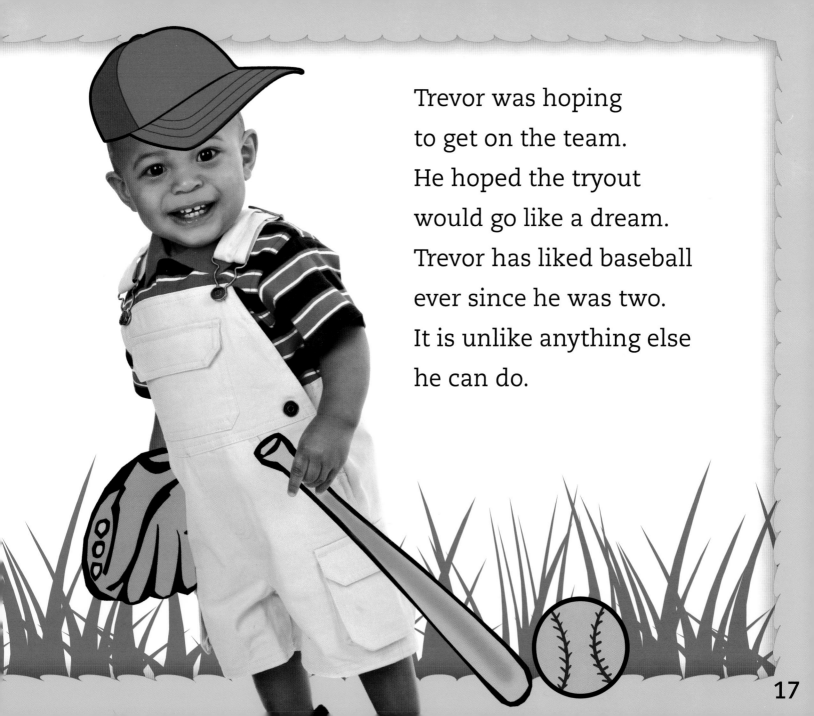

Trevor was hoping
to get on the team.
He hoped the tryout
would go like a dream.
Trevor has liked baseball
ever since he was two.
It is unlike anything else
he can do.

Tryout day finally came, and Trevor was tense.
But on his final swing, the ball flew over the fence!
Then Coach said, "Try playing shortstop, Trevor."
And Trevor showed him he was the
best player ever.

Trevor made the team and said,
"Coach, I am thankful indeed!"
Coach said, "Doing your best is all
the thanks that I need.
You can help this team win.
I know I'm not wrong.
You won't be an unknown
ballplayer for long!"

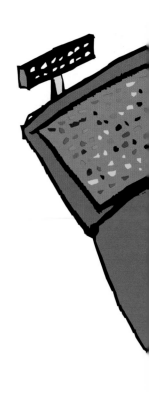

Match It Up!

Choose the word with the correct prefix or suffix to complete each sentence.

1 Tracy stops to _____ her shoe.
   a. ties
   b. retie

2 Randy is _____ down the field.
   a. rerun
   b. running

3 Mary Jo really enjoys _____.

    a. winning

    b. winner

4 Jim wears a helmet to be _____.

    a. unsafely

    b. safe

5 Wade _____ at the pitcher when he is up to bat.

    a. looks

    b. looking

Glossary

adjective (p. 7) – a word used to describe someone or something. Tall, green, round, happy, and cold are all adjectives.

meaning (pp. 4, 5) – the idea or sense of something said or written.

noun (p. 9) – a word that is the name of a person, place, or thing.

opposite (pp. 7, 13) – being completely different from another thing.

shortstop (p. 18) – a baseball or softball player who stands between second and third base.

trophy (p. 10) – a prize given to the winner of a competition.

verb (pp. 7, 9) – a word for an action. Be, do, think, play, and sleep are all verbs.